I0023248

Memória VIVA

"WHEN A FIGHTING WOMAN DIES, WE ALL DIE A LITTLE WITH HER."[1]

Tecnhical Information

Disclaimer

About the Book

It was March 14, 2018. Shots rang out on that hot, summer night. Just another night in Rio, had it not been for the victim, councilwoman Marielle Franco, gunned down brutally, as she returned home from an event only a few miles away. The perpetrator? That's the question that two years later has no response.

Memória Viva explores the legacy of councilwoman Franco through the prism of the streets. It examines the pixação and graffiti art that have helped keep her memory alive, while joining the chorus for justice. "Quem mandou matar Marielle?" and "Marielle Presente" are two of the rallying cries scattered around the city, demanding answers and justice. But as the investigations continue and another anniversary of her death approaches, the questions remain. But the streets don't forget, and this outpouring of love and support reflect the impact of Marielle on this city. Memória Viva presents over 200 impactful images collected since March 14, 2018.

About Aerosol Carioca

Aerosol Carioca was founded in 2010 with the intent of documenting Rio de Janeiro's vandalism and urban art scene. Since its launch, Aerosol Carioca has been one of Rio de Janeiro's most ardent graffiti advocates. "Memória Viva" is its third publication

Contact Info
IG: @aerosolcarioca
aerosolcarioca@gmail.com

Layout and Design: skddesign
IG: @sofakingdopedesign
ISBN 978-65-00009-29-3

Table of Contents 3

Dedication

to the victims of violence
everywhere.

Anderson

QUEM MANDOU MA

14 de março de 2019
Um ano de luta por justiça para Marielle e Anderson

"WHAT DOES IT MEAN TO BE A WOMAN? WHAT HAS EACH OF US STOPPED DOING OR HAS DONE WITH SOME LEVEL OF DIFICULTY BECAUSE OF OUR GENDER IDENTITY, BECAUSE WE ARE WOMEN?"

MARIELLE PRESENTE, HOJE E SEMPRE!

BEFORE THE WORD

As I write these words I find myself still hesitant about writing anything on the topic of Marielle Franco. There are many people out there, including her family, friends and colleagues, who would be more appropriate at speaking about her life and work.

However, my intent was never to speak on her, specifically, but on how the streets have kept her memory alive. And that to me has been fascinating to see. As I reflected and organized the images in this book I realized that the memory of Marielle isn't important just for her family, but for the hundreds of victims of violence whose deaths are rarely, if ever solved. That's why keeping alive the memories of the victims of violence is so important, and using the streets as a microphone to call out injustices when we see them is a tool we need to become even more comfortable with.

In the days after Marielle's assasination I noticed that there were many people who understood the connection between the streets and collective memory. While researching for the book *"Graffiti City: Art and Vandalism on the Streets of Rio,"* I would walk around the city, taking pictures. One day I began to notice the Marielle focused graffiti art and pixação throughout the city. At first I thought nothing of it, but I began to reflect on the importance of those manifestations in the local context and how calling for justice for Marielle, and others, through street art and vandalism, was probably the most carioca thing to do. So I decided to put those images together in one place, to let the world see how the streets are keeping her memory alive.

My goal was, and continues to be, defending and motivating artists, storytellers, vandals, citizens and anyone who feels like it to step out onto the streets and use city walls as a way to manifest their humanity. Whether it be a scribble, a name, a mural, a poster or just a simple picture, each manifestation on the streets is a connection between people and a society that is constantly distancing itself from each other.

Unlike other projects on the subject, I decided to write as little as possible and let the images speak for themselves. It was the only way I knew to let the magnitude of it all penetrate those who pick up this book. My focus will always be the streets. A place of glaring contradictions and where in the midst of the chaos is one of the few places where I can find peace of mind.

Though I have written a short history about pixação and graffiti art in Rio de Janeiro, I've done so in order for readers to understand how important the memorial art and vandalism is within the local context.

My hope is that this book, and the *Aerosol Carioca* project, serve as a testament to the importance of dialogue and how the streets, as an original social media platform, serve as a place where the theater of life plays itself out, honestly, with no filter. Though Marielle is not the first, nor the last person gunned down violently, her memory is etched into the consciousness of this city with each message written on the walls. Is the memory of Marielle Franco as valuable as her physical presence, no, but her memory is more valuable than the void left without it.

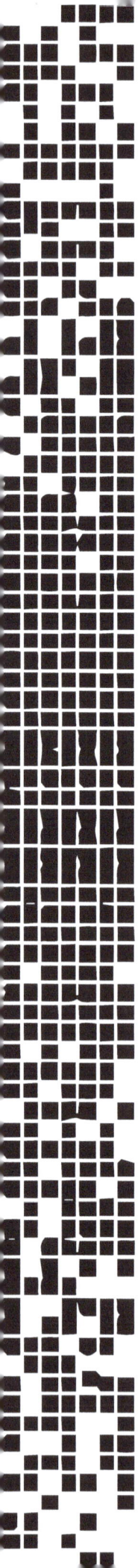

INTRO

Much of the research into Rio's graffiti art and pixação cultures place their genesis in the years after the installation of the military regime, in 1964. Those who support this line of thinking point to the battle cry "down with the dictatorship" (Abaixo Ditadura) as the singular phrase that launched pixação into the public consciousness. Others point to the Parisian protests of 1968 as being responsible for the dissemination of pixação throughout Brazilian cities. In reality, a much more complicated historical process created the environment for pixação's birth decades before the installation of the 1964 regime.

Wall writing as a form of communication has been historically linked to various cultures. Though techniques have differed intent has always been the same: to leave a legacy, mark territory and to make a statement. This is the motivating factor for wall writing in Rio de Janeiro in the early 20th century. During this period wall writing was relatively common in Rio de Janeiro as a simple and inexpensive form of local advertising for commercial goods and services. This practice is still common throughout the city today. But mass European immigration through the late 1930s, appropriation of public space for dialogue in the 1940s and the implementation of repressive policies during the military dictatorship in the 1960s laid the foundation for a national urban arts movement that began during the 1970s, and flourished in the 1980s, 1990s and 2000s.

Top: Clarice Lissovsky
Bottom: Dani Fi

13

ATÉ

uno debize
eitos human
arielle

Por um
Marielle presente

V
I
karine guerra

MARIELLE vive

PRETAS
em
LUTA

NI UN
MINUTO
DE SILENCI
SU VOZ
SU LUCHA
SU COMPRO
SU AMO
SIGUEN

15

SOBRELOJA
QUEM MATOU
MARIELE FRANCO?
ELE NÃO
ELE NÃO!
LULA
ELE NÃO!

MARIELLE PRESENTE

QUARTA 30/05

SIMPLE PLAN

QUINTA 31/05

ANGRA
MAIEUTICA

MARIELLE PRESENTE

17

MARIELL

PRESENT

#LutoÉVerbo

UME!

SEN

SCANDAL!

ministeriodaverdade

21

carioca graffiti: a brief history

Rio de Janeiro at the turn of the 20th century was a burgeoning metropolis. The establishment of the First Republic, in 1889, brought with it seismic social and political changes reflected in the growth of urban centers in Brazil's southeastern region. In Rio de Janeiro, Mayor Pereira Passos' reimagination of the city was in full course and a once small city center was expanding through rapid and aggressive urbanization. This period also saw an increase in the number of literate Brazilians, which was reflected in a boom of sign making to sell products, deliver messages and announce political candidacies.

In spite of public outcry over the visual pollution that signs caused advertisers roamed the city in the calm of the night, and with no hesitation placed their signs where they pleased. There were laws in place that prohibited this, namely *Art. 88 of the City Code*, but there was little the city government could or wanted to do to deal with this problem.

So rampant was the political advertisement that a new term *"os eleitos da piche"* (politicians elected due to their use of piche) was coined.

A September 1929 article in the *Jornal de Nictheroy* highlights how unauthorized signs also plagued that city and as a responce residents began to remove them. Unfortunately, in looking to resolve one problem they unwittingly created another one that would plague both cities for the next 70 years:

"City of Posters: Although there is a formal prohibition on the placement of posters on the walls and walls of houses, the city is full of scribbles and full of advertisements. In order for them not to be removed advertisers, instead of posting ads on paper, began to use ink and often tar!"

This article potentially points to that moment when wall writing becomes a phenomenon in Rio. As advertisers looked for ways to guarantee their ads were seen, and not removed, they inadvertently repurposed city walls. Combined with the Maggioli incident vandalism of 1910, the conscious move to write directly on walls was revolutionary. In just a few short years wall writing was out of control, and public ordinances to impede its spread were almost completely ignored.

Beginning in 1946, students including those associated with the União Nacional de Estudantes (UNE), land reformers and laborers continued this tradition, painting dissent messages on walls protesting the unstable political and economic climate of Brazil's Second Republic. But the UNE's portrayal as a communist organization brought with it condemnation from a society caught in the paranoia of the "red scare"

Amid political demonstrations that swept Brazil in the early 1960s pichação's visibility increased, but now it wasn't just leftist protestors exploring the use of pixação. The first paramilitary group in Brazil, the *Anticommunist Movement* (MAC), was created in Rio de Janeiro, in 1961, with the aim of fighting the "red danger". The MAC was created as a response to president João Goulart's decision to resume diplomatic relations with the Soviet Union. Though the MAC morphed into a violent, extremist, right-wing armed militia, eventually partnering with the *Comando de Caça aos Comunistas* (CCC), in its first months the group vandalized several buildings around Rio. Some of their slogans included *"Morte aos traidores Prestes e Julião"*, *"Fuzilemos brasileiros, os lacaios de Moscou"*, *"Fogo nos comunistas"* and *"Guerra de morte ao PCB"*. The use of pichação by both MAC and UNE, who's headquarters were vandalized by MAC pichos in January 1962, show how pichação was part of the Brazilian social context independent of political orientation.

In the 1970s, pichadores and protestors were actively present on the streets, but now hippies, poets and even religious groups began marking walls in major cities for a variety of reasons. Whether political or personal, pichação's spread was aided by an urban decay that defined Brazil in that era. This spread coincided with the *"Anos de Chumbo"* (1968-1974), the most repressive years of the regime, unofficially "coming to an end". The transition signaled a partial dismantling of AI-5 and freedoms being slowly re-established. This was evidenced by the resurgence of campaign pichação by mainstream candidates. An O Globo article from April 25, 1976 titled *"Candidatos já picham muros em Niterói"* and a follow up article on April 26, 1976 titled *"Corregedor diz que pichar muros é crime eleitoral,"* highlight that throughout 1976 pichação was increasingly used by establishment politicians. Campaign pichação was met head on by protest pichação, and throughout the decade politically oriented pichadores made use of the public space with little concern for the consequences.

It wasn't until 1977 that a culture of pichação first emerged in Rio. During this period Carioca pichadores quickly multiplied due to the appearance of two phrases: *"Celacanto Provoca Maremoto"*, by Carlos Alberto Teixeira, and *"Lerfa Mu,"* by Guilherme Jardim and Rogério Fornari. These phrases ignited an aggressive spread of pichação in Rio due to the media attention they garnered. For months Cariocas theorized about Celacanto's and Lerfa Mu's origins. *Was Celacanto a communist battlecry? Was it subversive code? Was it leftist revolutionary propaganda?* It turned out both pichos were the creation of teenage boys, as Teixeira admitted to in a 1977 newspaper article.

Celacanto and Lerfa Mu were turning points for Carioca pichação as it migrated towards less political incarnations and moved towards a culture focused on self expression. During this period traditional artists, inspired by the subversion of the public sphere, began putting color markings on walls and experimented with alternatives that could take advantage of inroads achieved by pichação. In retrospect, Celacanto and Lerfa Mu accomplished three things: First, they propagated pichação's first big boom. Secondly, they shifted pichação's focus from politics to self affirmation through enigmatic expression. Finally, they introduced the idea of a "crew", in addition to the competitiveness that is the centerpiece of today's pixação culture.

Public intrigue on the national and local level lead to newspapers publishing articles questioning "Celacanto" and "Lerfa Mu's" purpose. This curiosity inspired new pichadores with markings inked by poetic individuals spreading rapidly throughout the city. Unknowingly, this generation of Carioca pichadores asserted an egocentric focus to their pichação in an era known as "pichação poética". But they were simultaneously creating the foundations for the 'xarpi' subculture that would emerge in the 1980s. Pichação poetica existed in contrast to pichação's political context, and was stylistically different from what was going on in São Paulo, as evidenced in Pedro Camargo's 1979 short film *"Celacanto Provoca Lerfa Mú"*. This film beautifully documented the burgeoning Carioca pichação culture through interviews with contemporary pichadores. His film captured the various techniques used, and highlighted the tags of some of Rio's most well-known pichadores including *Jes, Jan, Brucutú, Paorje, Megalodon, Origi, Pitú, Nature, Eggs, Aspen, Cibié, Moanga Rosa* and *Rato*.

Looking to curb pichação's spread acting mayor Marcos Tamoio (1975-1979) implemented new fines for anyone caught vandalizing. But Tamoio's light punishment and the media attention towards Celacanto/Lerfa Mu only motivated new pichadores. Writers like Tildro, Creca, Esmeril, Fig and others were appearing daily. So impactful were Celacanto's and Lerfa Mu's messages that they were transformed into marketing campaigns. A famous adaptation of the phrase was by the appliance store "Bemoreira", which created the slogan: *"Celacanto Provoca Maremoto de Preços"*. In 1978, the DPZ advertising firm referenced "Lerfa

Mu" in an ad that ran in local newspapers, and in the Tijuca neighborhood, at the Praça Saens Pena, a store named "Celacanto" sold youth fashion with the phrase *"do grafismo às vitrines"*. An opportune use of urban poetry was a sign of things to come as the appropriation of urban visual language for capital gains would be the norm decades later.

The early 1980s saw graffiti art and pichação slowly being distinguished from one another, as one was considered art and the other being labeled as vandalism. In the eyes of many the main difference was that graffiti art was seen as something at the very least personal, while pichação was seen as a political manifestation or malicious destruction. This distinction was due in part to the arrival of US American hip hop movies, which introduced an alternative urban manifestation to which pichação could be compared to.

In 1983, the films *Wild Style* and *Style Wars* hit Carioca theaters and signaled the beginning of Rio's hip hop history. These releases were followed by the 1984 releases of *Beat Street* and *Breakdance*, and the 1985 release of *Krush Groove*. Initially, hip hop's popularity was considered a fad. Part of this was because of racial implications as hip hop was an unapologetically black, urban manifestation. For a country unwilling to deal with its racism it made it hard to reimagine hip hop in an alternative prism. Hip hop's association with street culture, which seemed to give pichação a reinvigoration, frustrated authorities. But hip hop wasn't a fad. Its cultural influence was immediate. By 1984 the word graffiti (alternatively grafite) was common in the local lexicon, and a conversation about graffiti art versus pichação took new directions.

Brazilian youth consumed all things hip hop,

especially in middle class neighborhoods, and together with a reinvigorated interest in skateboard culture created a market for US urban culture. Films, music videos and magazines that chronicled the hip hop, graffiti and US skateboard scenes became sought after commodities. They evolved into cultural access points. This was hugely important in a country that was slowly undoing itself from the chains of censorship imposed from 1964 to 1985.

Hip Hop exploded in Rio de Janeiro in 1993. MV Bill and DJ Sergio Tr, trailblazers in the city's Hip Hop movement, started the first community Hip Hop radio station, *SOS Consciência*, in the Cidade de Deus neighborhood. Hip Hop spread quickly through Rio's favelas and groups like Filhos do Gueto and Artigo 288 gained large followings in Rio's underground. Artists like Ademir Lemos, Geração Futuro, Def Yuri, Damas do Rap, Gabriel o Pensador, Contagem Regressiva, Poetas de Ébano and others were pioneering this new wave, turning an international sound into a local one. *Tiro Inicial*, the first Carioca hip hop album, was released in 1993, and soon after producer Elza Cohen started organizing Hip Hop shows at Fundição Progresso, in Lapa. This boom intensified a consumption of all things Hip Hop, especially graffiti art. Again, it was through hip hop that graffiti art was able to solidify its place within the city's cultural context. As the 90s progressed graffiti's influence in Rio de Janeiro grew exponentially, as did pixação's. While artists used graffiti's growing acceptance to create new cultural an economic opportunities for the genre, pixadores and activists continued attacking the city's social and political consciousness with their appropriation of the public space for dialogue. This dichotomy continues today, and is an important element of the city's cultural identity. Though done in different ways, both graffiti and pixação are tools that express collective thoughts.

Today, graffiti art is a powerful force on the streets and within the city's numerous favelas despite its aggressive "elitization". But this only occurs when graffiti is in the hands of those who are truly willing to explore its revolutionary elements of protest and humanization. This is especially true for graffiti art done in the suburbios and favelas through initiatives organized by the grafiteiros. But the graffiti art needed for this is another type of graffiti art. A peripheral graffiti art, far from the reaches of commercial interests. A graffiti art that creates a dialogue with the community it exists in.

Walking these streets for the last six years has taught me that neither art nor vandalism is without context. Pixação and graffiti art are always the response to something. We are political beings. Our actions and what we create are political. Defiance in resisting and existing is a political act. Art is then a political statement, by definition. Art isn't synonymous with the beautiful. It is not an accepted aesthetic. It should never be. Art is synonymous with being. With expression. With humanity. Art is a way to live within repressive systems. A humanizing factor in a dehumanizing world. It is the desire to be human even in a context when the basic notion of humanity is being questioned and protested. Thus, it is not about defending vandalism. It is understanding that people have voices that need to be heard. It is about understanding that art and humanity come in all varieties.

QUEM MATOU MARIELLE?

QUEM MANDOU O AMIGO DO PRESIDENTE MATAR MARIELE?

Sabemos quem MATOU MARIELE

FEMINICIDADE

"Quantos mais vão precisar morrer pra que essa guerra acabe?"

FEMINICIDADE

FEMINICIDADE

"Quantos mais vão precisar morrer pra que essa guerra acabe?"

CHICO

MARIELE

Foto: George Wilson

29

OS MAIS VÃO
AR MORRER
QUE ESSA
RA ACABE?

NOSS
VIDA
IMPORT

PAREM
DE MATAR
A POPULAÇÃO
NEGRA

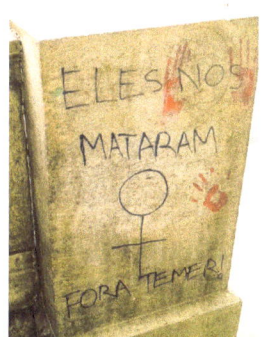

#mariellepre

MPANHEIRA
ARIELLE
RESENTE
RESENTE
RESENTE

PARE
DE MAT
A POPULAÇ
NEGR

Nessa semana que jovens
foram mortos e jogados em
um valão (em Acari)
Hoje a população negra
ameaçando os m

Marielle Franco
PRESENTE

MARIELLE VIVE

ACAB

MARIELLE
PRESENTE

A REVOLUÇÃO
VIRÁ DAS FAVELA
ELES NOS
MATARAM

PRESENTE   PRESENTE   PRESENTE

LUTO
BANGU
RESISTE

ELES NOS
MATARAM
LUTO
FORA TEMER

NA FAVELA
TEM VITM
TODO DIA

ELES NOS
MATARA

MARIELLE
PRESENTE

LUTO

AREM
MATAR
PULAÇÃO
EGRA

#FORAFASCISTAS
Marielle
PRESENTE

DE
REIRO
ORA
ELLE FRANCO
OL-RJ)
DA RELATORA
MISSÃO QUE
ACOMPANHAR A
ERVENÇÃO NO
RJ.

10 DE
MARÇO
MARIELLE
DENUNCIA
VIOLENCIA
POLICIAL
EM
ACARI.

DE
REIRO
ORA
ELLE FRANCO
OL-RJ)
DA RELATORA
MISSÃO QUE
COMPANHAR A
ERVENÇÃO NO
RJ.

10 DE
MARÇO
MARIELLE
DENUNCIA
VIOLENCIA
POLICIAL
EM
ACARI.

14
M
MA
E
A

PRESENTE

FORA
TEMER

MARIELLE PRESE

ONDE A TIRANIA É L

NTE

LI A REVOLTA É AORDEM

OVIVE!
POVO NEGRO VIVE
LE!
NÃO A INTERVENSÃO

STADO RACISTA
MARIELLE VIV
DA PM JÁ!!

ACOI
EMOCRACIA E UMA FARSA! ES
FAVELA É LUGAR DE PAZ

BLACK
POER

MARIELLE
VIVE
VIVA
ZAPATA

MARIELLE
FILHA DA
LUTA

GOLPE

ESTADO ASSASSINO!

MARIELLE PRESENTE!

foi crime
serra poesia

POR
MARIELLE!

RESENTE   PRESENTE

FORA
TEMER

EU SOU
PORQUE NÓS SOMOS
MARIELLE
VIVE

Marielle Franco
PRESENTE

ANDERSON PRESENTES/ HO

MARIELLE GIG

MARIELLE VIVE!

EU SOU PORQUE NÓS SOMOS

UMA, L
TRÊS F
MAS JA
ETERÃ
IN

MARIELLE
VIVE
NINGUÉM
CALARÁ

MARIELLE

Amarildo, Rafael Braga,
Gabriel Pereira Alves, Lucas
Monteiro dos Santos,
Tiago Freitas, Dy
Xavier de Brit
Jesus Viegas Menezes
Júnior, Ma reth Teixeira,
Roberto de za, Carl
Eduardo da Souza,
Cleiton Cor de Souza, Wesley
Castro, e Wi n Esteves
Domingos J nior, Rodrigo
Alexandre da Silva

MEMORIA *VIVA*

The city's walls allow us to explore collective history and memory, or ask difficult questions we want answers to. There is an impact in using the city canvas as a way to remember those who have passed, and guarantee they will not be forgotten. The city's walls have also been ground zero for calls to action and the vindication of collective rights. The assassination of Assemblywoman Marielle Franco, on March 14, 2018, the fight for the pardoning of Raphael Braga and demands to find Amarildo Dias de Souza have been three high profiled cases that have used the streets as a space to continue the dialogue once the media attention had subsided. But it's not just political personalities that are remembered on the streets. Community leaders, activists, cultural icons, victims of violence, local heroes or family friends are forever immortalized on Rio's walls. It is the power of wall writing. Though the state chooses its heroes as a way to legitimize its perception amongst the citizenry, when citizens choose their own heroes and take control of the public space they challenge the state's monopoly on defining who gets remembered, and how. In many ways this form of graffiti is a form of resistance in tangible and non-tangible ways.

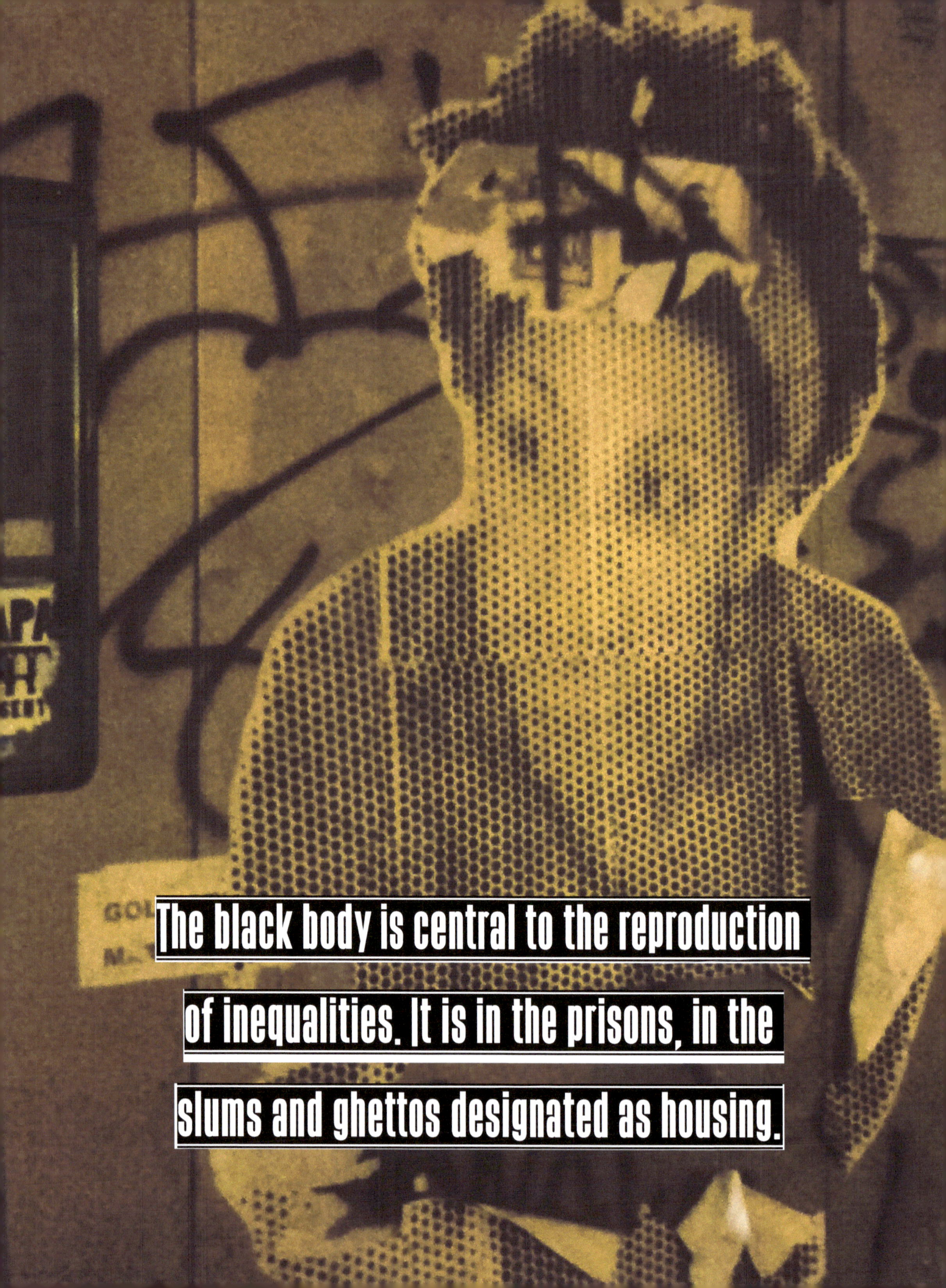

The black body is central to the reproduction of inequalities. It is in the prisons, in the slums and ghettos designated as housing.

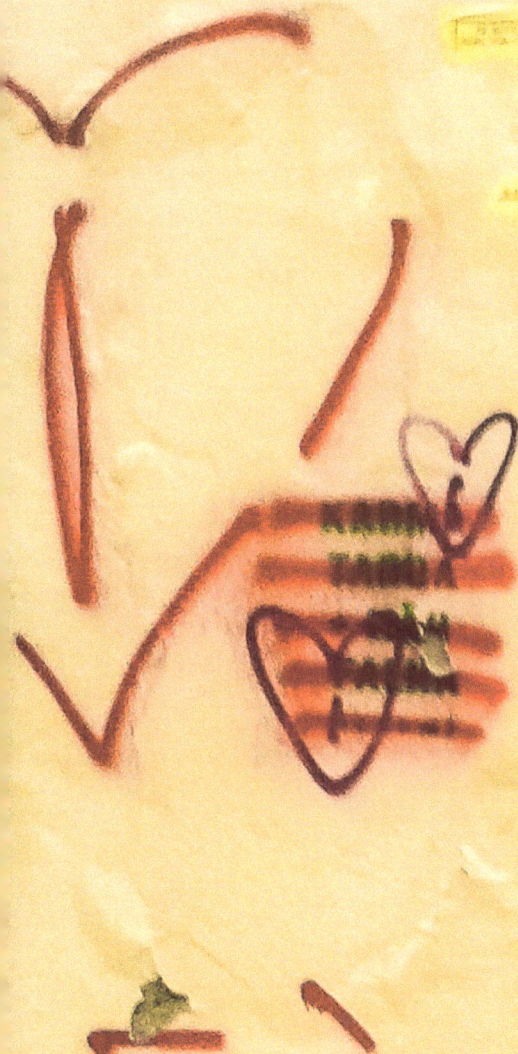

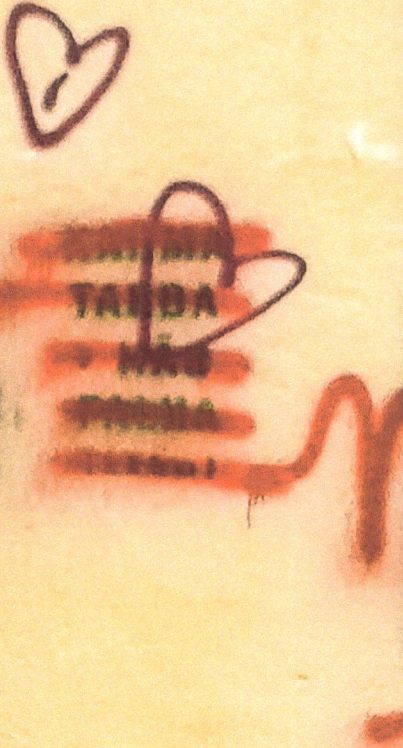

ÃO A INTERVENÇÃ
MILITAR

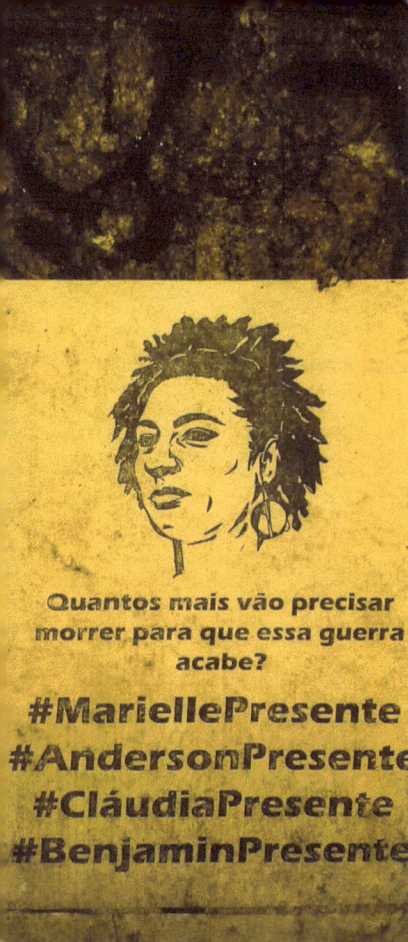

Quantos mais vão precisar morrer para que essa guerra acabe?

#MariellePresente
#AndersonPresente
#CláudiaPresente
#BenjaminPresente

LESBICAS P.B MARIELLE

MARIELLE PRESENTE HOJE E SEMPRE

FEMINICIDADE

A VERDADE SOBRE

A VERDADE SOBRE MARIELLE

QUEM MATOU MARIELLE

COMPANHEIRA, ME AJUDA
QUE EU NÃO POSSO
ANDAR SÓ
EU SOZINHA ANDO BEM
MAS COM VOCÊ
ANDO MELHOR

COM MARI

MARIELLE FRANCO PRESENTE

MARIELLE presente

MARIELLE VIVE

ERDEMOS INCLUSIVE O M

#BlackLivesMatter

tos mais

tecisar MORR

que

guerra

ABE?

JESU

MARI VIVE!

MARIELLE presente

MARIELL presente

45

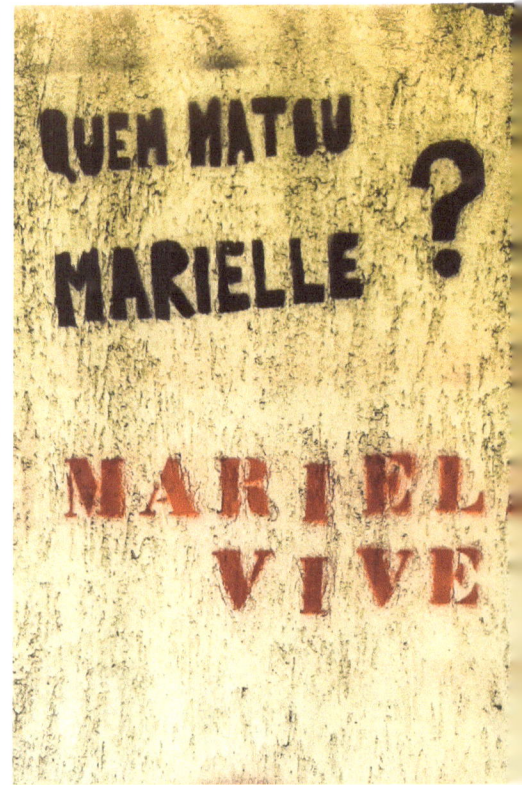

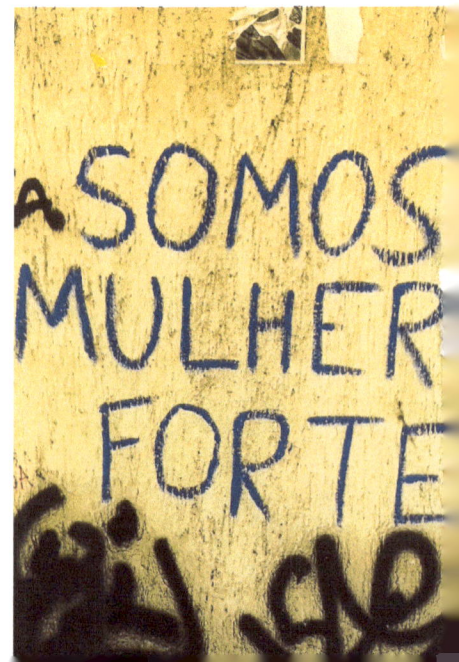

LUTO
LUTA

OMOS
OLXS
RIELLE
#MARI
PRESO

MARIELLE VIVE!
LUTE
COMO UMA
MARIELLE

ONTINUAREMO
TUA LUTA

MARIELLE
VIVE

ANONIMITY

There is strength in numbers. There is also strength in anonymity. The streets are a haven for pixadores, grafiteiros, vandals, artists and free thinkers looking to express personal and collective ideas. Revolutionary ideas about toppling authoritarian governments. Mundane ideas about last night's dinner. Ridiculous ideas about the benefits of neoliberalism. They all find a place on Rio's walls.

But more than a stage for the free flow of ideas, the streets provide vandals anonymity. Protection to express a variety of opinions, without the fear of retribution. We see it daily on our social media feeds. People expressing opinions and in the blink of an eye the swell of hate that can explode. Threats of digital violence have become the norm as a false sense of anonymity emboldens the hate. But, unlike the internet, those who venture on to the streets to declare what they please are protected by the moment they paint in. Their ideas stay behind, long after, dismissing the notion of ephemeral art, and highlighting the importance of having a safe space to exist and coexist with people, and their ideas, without fear of reprisal. In this moment, there is a dialogue between the writer and the message. And then, for as long as the messages stay up on walls, there is a dialogue between writer, message and recipient, even if the recipient isn't cognizant of it, or willing to accept the dialogue. And there is no one you can yell at if you disagree. It's just you and the emotions the message evoke within you.

So, in a world where ideas are dangerous, where ideas merit execution, where the audacity to voice can get you killed, anonymity is protection.

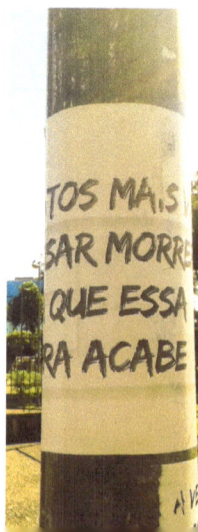

MARIELLE VIVE!

EU SOU PORQUE NÓS SOMOS

#LULA LIVRE

VOLTA DILMA! ANULA O GOLPE!

MARIELLE

PODERÃO CORTAR UMA FLOR

MAS NÃO PODERÃO DETER A PRIMA

PRESENTE

MARIELLE

53

A MANDOU **MATAR** MA

MARIELLE VIVE!

EU SOU PORQUE NÓS SOMOS

MARIELLE VIVE!

OCUPE POR MARIELLE

MARIELLE
PRESENTE
HOJE E
SEMPRE

"Rape culture is
a real problem,
and between the
saintly and the
profane,
I prefer the
empowerment of
women.
Of all women."

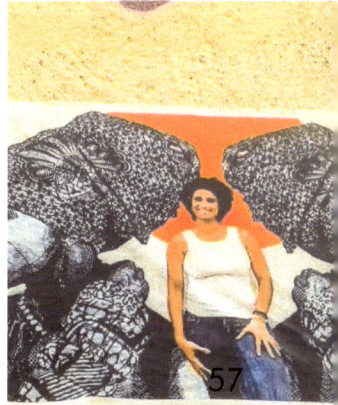

QUANTOS MAIS TEM
MORRER PRA ESSA
ATÉ QUANDO? ACAB
ANDERSON PRE

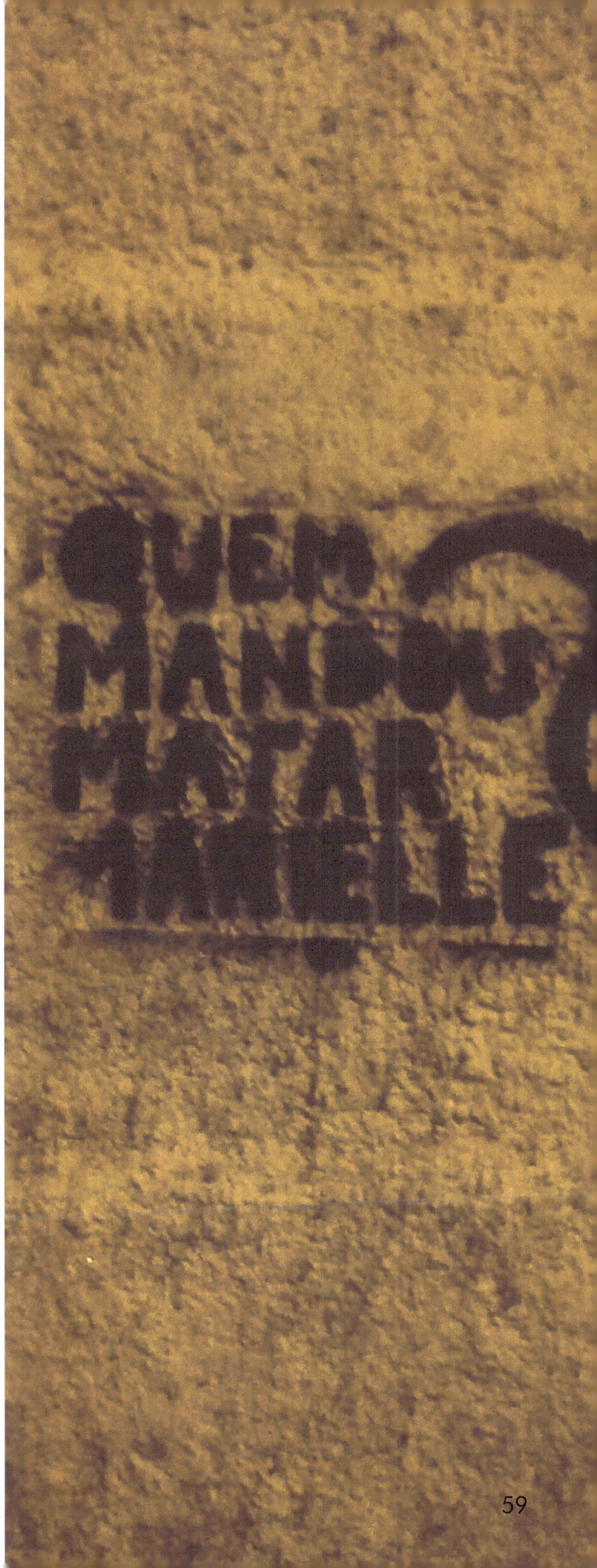

QUE
GUERRA
AR?

QUEM
MANDOU
MATAR
MARIELLE?

THE POLITICS OF
HATE

Brazil has returned to its former self. A Brazil where ideas are dangerous and where some people have to be "put in their place", even if by force.

Politics in Brazil are less about ideas that move society forward, and more about the ressurgence of ideologues who are scared that hope is a dangerous concept that must be squashed at all costs. Thirty four years of progress gone in a matter of months. Cynics would say that the 2018 presidential elections didn't turn back the clock, rather they forced Brazilians to understand that progress hadn't been reached through three decades of struggle. That in fact all the progress of the previous 34 years was all done on borrowed time. That at some point Brazil would revert back to its old self. And the reversion is occurring with a hateful vengeance. A Brazilian dominating class, angered that Brazil's oppressed classes had an abundance of hope in those 34 years, decided to take back what they thought was rightfully theirs, and began a campaign of uprooting any and every semblance of progress, even if it meant cutting off their own hands in the process.

There have been few periods in Brazilian history of relative political peace, but the 34 years since the end of the dictatorship provided Brazilians with some semblance of democracy that they have not quite gotten used to. With this newly acquired democracy came the idea of plurality that many Brazilians didn't really know how to deal with. It wasn't just new voices and opinions, but what those voices were saying and what they were demanding: equality and equity. This caused a clash of ideas that in typical Brazilian fashion was ignored. But the arrival of the internet and social media vehicles have only highlighted what outsiders have observed since its inception: a highly fractured nation still unwilling to face its past, which inevitably stifles any advances in the future.

And in the crevices of those fractures has emerged *the politics of hate*, which has framed the last 34 years, and specifically the 8 years of ex-President Lula's presidency, as a disastrous attempt at plurality and democracy. Emboldened in an era where white supremacy and nationalism have been unapologetically accepted into the mainstream political discourse, no longer cowering in the shadows of the political spectrum, the politics of hate have become a new normal. If in previous years the discourse was disguised in euphemisms and decorum, somewhat moralizing the hate and obfuscating its real intent, today, it is out in the open. The masks are literally and figuratively off with the only solution being to resist its spread.

MARIELLE VIVE!
MILITARIZAÇÃO:
NÃO EM NOSSO NOME!
MARIELLE
PRESENTE HOJE E SEMPRE!

VI
VE

PELE
10

#WONKLA

Marielle
vive

GREJAS PERTURBAM SONO DE DEUS

MARIELLE VIVE

MARIELLE APOIAVA Aborto.... AbortARAM ELA

Anti-Marielle vandalism: "Marielle supported abortion...she was aborted."

"AS ROS.. RESISTÊNCIA NA.. EM NO ASFALTO. A G..NTE RECEBE ROSAS, MAS VAMOS ESTAR COM O PUNHO CERRADO ..LANDO DE NOSSA ..NCIA CONTRA O.. ..MANDOS E DESMANDOS C.. ..TAM NOSSAS ..

MARIELLE VIV..

MARIELLE VIVE!

EU SOU PORQUE NÓS SOMOS

the scene

On the night of March 14, 2018, Marielle Franco was returning home after participating in the *"Jovens Negras Movendo Estruturas"* (Young Black Women Changing Structures) event in Rio's Lapa neighborhood. The councilwoman was urging other young black woman to do what she was trying to do: *change structures*. And it was this desire to change structures that made her a target. She was trafficking in the most lethal drug in the political sphere: hope. She was making waves, making friends and making enemies. She was fearless, though. It was a fight she had prepared herself for. She understood the risks she was facing, but moved forth because she cared about the causes and the people it was affecting. This was what endeared her to supporters and what angered detractors.

Franco's election to the city council, in 2016, was not only surprising, but indicative of a change in the wind. Long imprisoned in the shadows of racism, homophobia and respectability politics candidates like Marielle, an openly gay, black woman who had a child out of wedlock in her teenage years, was a political and social outsider. But her election, having been the 5th most voted candidate in 2016 out of 1,500 potentials, proved that there was a place for her in public life, and that she had the popular support to challenge social structures. Human rights abuses, gay rights, police brutality, the police state and political corruption were among the issues Marielle worked on, but are also among the most problematic issues in the city's political spectrum because they directly challenge the authority of Rio's political structure.

If you didn't know who Marielle Franco was on March 13th, or what she stood for, that would all change on March 14th. Her death, though tragic and painful, would pull back the curtain on the extent to which violence had taken over the city, and who exactly held power in this city.

FAVELA É CIDADE

MARIELLE VIVE!

MARIELLE VI...

...O SOU PORQUE NÓS S...

QUANTOS MAIS VÃO PRECISAR MORRER PARA QUE ESSA GUERRA ACABE?

MARIELLE VIVE!

MARIELLE ERA E FAVELA

MARIELLE, PRESENTE

MARIELLE VIVE!

MARIELLE VIVE

NÃO VÃO NOS CALAR!

MARIELLE ERA FAVELA

LU LA LI VRE

Marielle ViVE! RUA

MARIELLE

QUEM MANDOU MATAR MARIELLE??

March 14th, 2018

Vereadora do PSOL, Marielle Franco é morta a tiros…" read one headline. *"Vereadora Marielle Franco é morta no Estácio…"* read another. *"Marielle", "Marielle", "Marielle". "Mataram a Marielle?" "Marielle?" "Marielle? Quem matou Marielle?"*

It was seemingly just another sweltering March night, when shots rang out at 9:30pm, on Rua João Paulo I, near the Estácio neighborhood. The sounds of glass shattering, screeching tires and bullets ricocheting would've been described as just another one of Rio's 2,700+ murders had it not been for the occupants of the bullet riddled white Chevrolet Agile. But the occupants weren't shady mob figures or dime a dozen gangsters.

On that fateful night Franco, her assistant and her driver, Anderson Gomes, drove past the Estácio Metro station, heading towards the Tijuca neighborhood.

Gomes, a doting father who was working as a driver to make a few extra bucks for his family, drove the car calmly as he had done on many other occasions. There was no panic. In the back seat, diagonal to the driver's seat, was councilwoman Franco, and to her left was her assistant, whose identity has been concealed for protective measures. As Gomes turned onto João Paulo I Avenue, a car pulled up behind Franco's, firing 9 shots from a semi-automatic weapon, four of which struck Marielle. Three in the head and one in the neck. Three bullets hit Gomes. Marielle and Gomes were killed instantly. The attack was brutal.

But before tears were shed it was clear that Franco's death, though tragic, was not an accident. It was, in fact, a clear message to anyone daring to challenge the criminal cartels that dominate Rio's political system. The crime was something out of a movie script.

In a matter of seconds her name became a rallying cry for millions, and her execution would send chills through Brazilian social and political circles for all the wrong reasons. In the wake of the gruesome murder, Franco's would become a household name. And its mention would trigger the most extreme of reactions from supporters and detractors. Franco's execution highlighted a rupture within Brazilian society that began with the engineered coup of then President Dilma Rouseff, and in some ways culminated in the death of Franco. And her gruesome murder would uncover ties to the cancerous power grab of the *militias*, who have infiltrated government that stretched into the upper echelons of government.

In the months after her murder evidence as to who killed Marielle began circulating. And if her murder wasn't enough, the mounting evidence, which pointed to the highest levels of the local, state and federal government served as a reminder: Brazil had regressed to its original state of chaos. Plurality, democracy and change were not things Brazilians were going to accept easily.

MARIELLE VIVE

MARIELLE PRESENTE, HOJE E SEMPRE!

MARIELLE PRESENTE

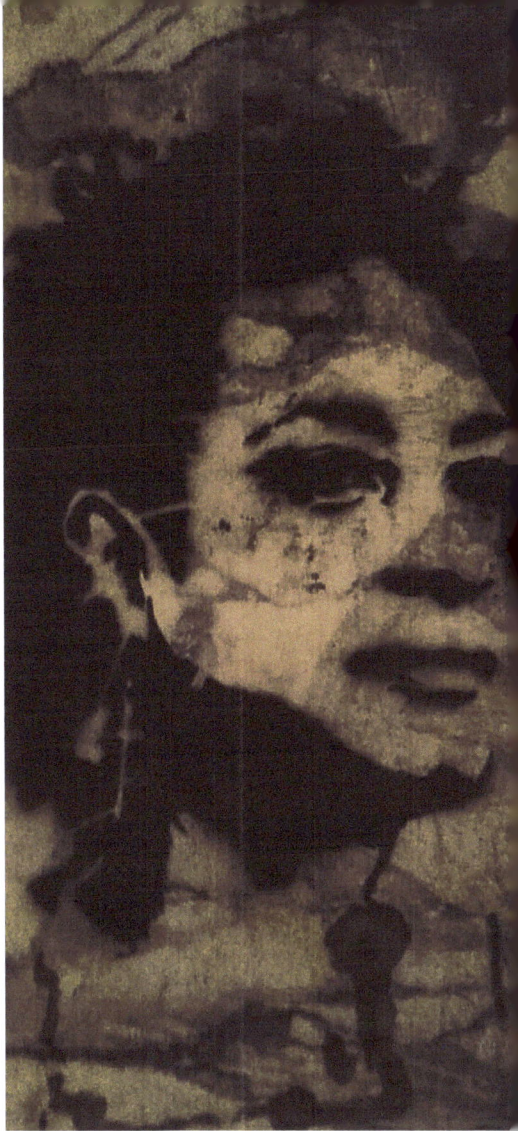

MARIELLE presente

MARIELLE VIVE!
LUTE
COMO UMA
MARIELLE

QUEM
MATOU
MARIELL

IMPORTAM?
IMPORTAM

A VERDADE
SOBRE
MARIELLE

#
MARIELLE
presente

MARIELLE
VIVE

Marielle

FORA
TEMER PRETO
VIVE!

MARIELLE

VIVE!

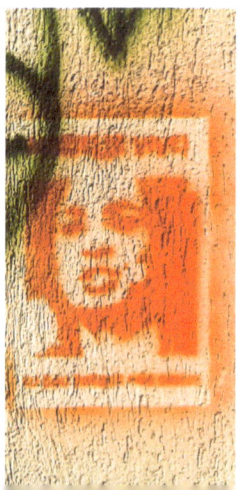

QUEM
MATOU
MARIELLE?

+CUIDADO
−SOLDADO

Quem
matou
MARIELLE

NÓS SOMOS PORQUE VOCÊ É

RUA

MARIELLE
PRESENTE
HOJE E SEMPRE!

"THEY WONT
SHUT US UP"

the aftermath

Investigations revealed the depth and sophistication of Marielle's execution. It was shocking. Though police maintained the investigations under wraps the little they did reveal pointed to a well planned conspiracy with the direct involvement of police and paramilitary police mafias known as *"milicias"*. Names of suspects began to circulate with each accusation more worrisome than the last.

As the days passed it became frustratingly clear that determining who was the orchestrator of this heinous crime was going to be a long, arduous task. Not because of the police's inability to investigate, but because of the interests that were directly connected to the murder.

But Marielle's supporters weren't going to let her be forgotten, and were determined to pressure officials to bring the perpetrators to justice. Protests and vigils were organized and spread to other Brazilians cities, and countries. The phrase *"Quem matou Marielle?"* became a rallying cry.

As the protests subsided and one murder headline replaced another, a curious thing happened. The streets began to honor Marielle. Mural art, lamb lambe's, chalk writing, tags, bombs, posters, stencils and other mediums were used by street artists and vandals to keep the conversation going. On wall after wall messages appeared with tributes to the councilwoman. On one hand the graffiti was helping to forge Marielle's legacy. On the other it was forcing us to look at what had become of Rio de Janeiro. It was a powerful statement to what Marielle meant to many, and exemplified the power of graffiti in this city. But there was more. It wasn't just that individuals were scribbling Marielle's name on walls, but that others were erasing those markings. In doing so they tried to erase the imaginative existence of Marielle from the social context. It was Rio's psyche playing out on the city's walls.

Two years after her untimely murder the question as to who ordered the hit on Marielle Franco remains unanswered. Theories abound as to who the shot caller(s) was, and a political chess match as to who will continue the investigation continues to diminish collective confidence that this will be solved any time soon.

But each new message scribbled onto a wall diminishes the possibility that she becomes just another statistic, because she has not been forgotten. As long as the walls reflect back to us her memory, and that of the thousands lost to violence each year, there is hope. And that is an invaluable currency.

In the aftermath Marielle's death and its investigation could provide this city positives in ways we have yet to imagine. Only perspective and time can give us that certainty. However, in the short term what has been interesting to consider is the gender of those who've been writing these messages. If the authors of the many messages have been women then it is a bold move to the streets, and a sign that women are demanding space in a traditionally male activity. And if it has been men calling for justice through graffiti art and pixação it is a positive sign that men are becoming more conscious of gender and gender violence issues, and are willing to speak out about them. And though we won't know for certain, both possibilities are necessary, and a tribute to Marielle's legacy.

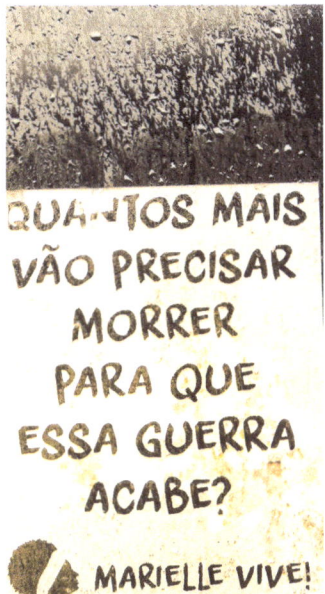

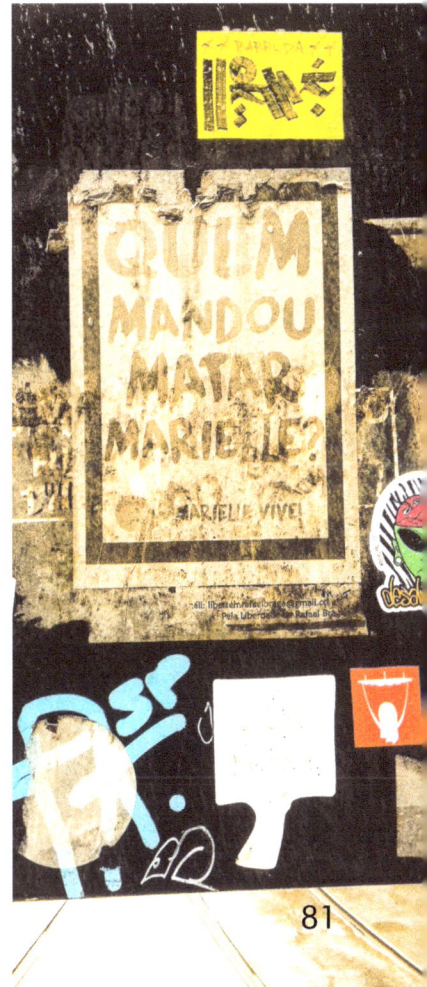

Rua
Marielle Franco

307   20260-080 Estácio

Rua
Marielle Franco
... Vereadora, defensora dos Direitos Humanos...
...
307   20260-080 Estácio

...lle Franco
...adora, defensora dos Di...
...ovardemente assassinada...
20260-080 Estácio

Foto credit:@landaramarcele
Artist: Aira Ocrespo

M.VINICIUS 14
MARIELLE 79

CRIME POLITICO?

BORDÔ BIELA

MARIELLE GIGANTE

MARIELLE VIVE

"THE BLACK BODY IS CENTRAL TO THE REPRODUCTION OF INEQUALITIES. IT IS IN THE PRISONS, IN THE SLUMS AND GHETTOS DESIGNATED AS HOUSING."

QUEM MATOU MARIELLE?

MARIELLE ERA = ANTICAPITALISTA

MARIELLE
PRESENTE

MARIELLE
PRESENTE

Marielle
presente

INTERVENÇÃO:
NÃO
EM NOSSO
NOME!

MARIELLE VIVE!

NÃO SEREMOS
INTERROMPIDAS!

MARIELLE VIVE!

QUEM MATOU
MARIELLE?

"Roses of resistance are born from asphalt. We nourish these roses, but our fists will be closed, voicing our existence against the rights and wrongs that affect our lives."

- Marielle Franco